# HEALING HEART
ORACLE

# HEALING HEART

## ORACLE

LOVE LETTERS TO YOUR SOUL

INNA SEGAL

Illustrated by Jena Dellagrottaglia

ROCKPOOL

A Rockpool book
PO Box 252
Summer Hill
NSW 2130
Australia

rockpoolpublishing.com
Follow us! **f** ◎ rockpoolpublishing
Tag your images with #rockpoolpublishing

ISBN: 9781922785381

Published in 2023 by Rockpool Publishing
Copyright text © Inna Segal 2023
Copyright illustrations © Jena Dellagrottaglia 2023
Copyright design © Rockpool Publishing 2023

All rights reserved. No part of this publication may be reproduced, stored in a retrieval system, or transmitted in any form or by any means, electronic, mechanical, photocopying, recording or otherwise without the prior written permission of the publisher.

Design and typesetting by Sara Lindberg, Rockpool Publishing
Edited by Lisa Macken

Printed and bound in China
10 9 8 7 6 5 4 3 2 1

# CONTENTS

INTRODUCTION ............................................................. 1

HOW TO USE THE CARDS ........................................ 3

THE CARDS ..................................................................... 11

01. HURT HEART: I see you ........................................................... 12

02. WORTHY HEART: you are enough ...................................... 14

03. UNSEEN HEART: you are significant .................................. 16

04. REBELLIOUS HEART: think for yourself ............................ 18

05. TRUSTING HEART: listen to your inner wisdom ............ 20

06. KNOWING HEART: heed your intuition ............................ 22

07. CURIOUS HEART: embark on a great adventure ............ 24

08. FEARFUL HEART: it's time to shine .................................... 26

09. DEEP HEART: believe in divine destiny ............................. 28

10. BETRAYED HEART: risk opening up to life and love ..... 30

11. CO-CREATIVE HEART: look for clear signs ..................... 32

12. RESILIENT HEART: it's time to rebuild ............................................ 34

13. GRIEVING HEART: open doors to something new ...................... 36

14. GIVING HEART: develop self-love ................................................... 38

15. HEALING HEART: face your shadow and grow ............................ 40

16. PASSIONATE HEART: use your voice to wake up others ............ 42

17. TRAPPED HEART: step outside your comfort zone ..................... 44

18. ADVENTUROUS HEART: set sail on a trip of a lifetime ............. 46

19. BEAUTIFUL HEART: open your wings and fly ............................. 48

20. DON'T GIVE UP ON LOVE HEART: what do you desire? .......... 50

21. FLIRTY HEART: have fun engaging your alluring nature ............. 52

22. CAUTIOUS HEART: have enough wisdom to get back up ......... 54

23. PATIENT HEART: move forward and grow .................................... 56

24. HUNGRY HEART: awaken the true song of your heart ............... 58

25. REMORSEFUL HEART: forgive and move ahead .......................... 60

26. RECOVERING HEART: step onto the road to deeper healing .. 62

27. HOPEFUL HEART: an exciting surprise is coming your way ..... 64

28. DARING HEART: learn to lead from wisdom ................................ 66

29. PROSPERING HEART: look for beauty, abundance and generosity ................................................................. 68

30. REINVENTING HEART: get to know yourself anew ................. 70

31. INTUITIVE HEART: step into your true destiny ........................... 72

32. LONGING HEART: value what you have and more will appear ................................................................................ 74

33. UNAVAILABLE HEART: face painful experiences and heal ........ 76

34. DIVINELY CONNECTED HEART: meet your karma ................... 78

35. REJECTED HEART: transform heartbreak into inner strength .... 80

36. FORGIVING HEART: don't let the past imprison you in the present ............................................................................. 82

# ACKNOWLEDGEMENTS 84

# ABOUT THE AUTHOR 85

# ABOUT THE ILLUSTRATOR 87

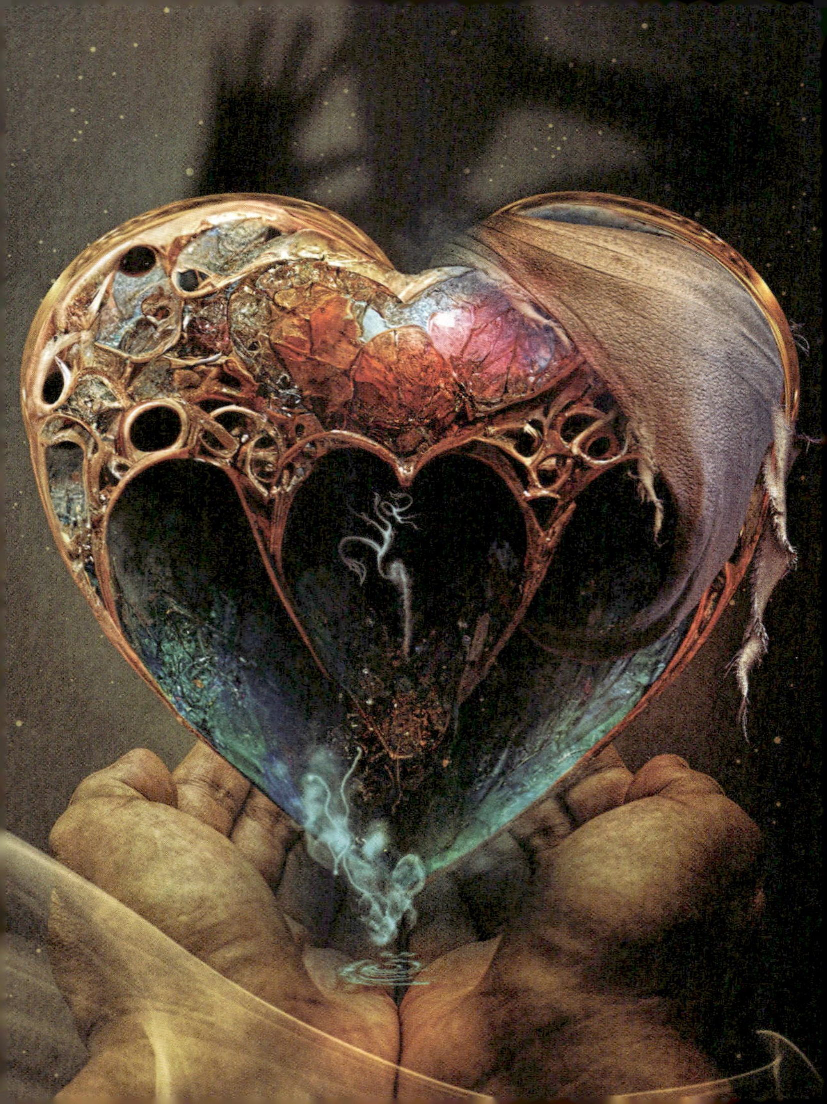

# INTRODUCTION

Pretty much every person who has interactions with others has felt rejected, hurt, confused, ignored or heartbroken at some point in their life. For me, the impulse to write heart-healing cards occurred during my separation from my husband: I felt that the best way I could support my heart to heal and strengthen was by writing love letters to each aspect of my heart that felt wounded. I also wanted to encourage the parts of my heart that felt stunted or frozen to revive and blossom. This was an extremely cathartic experience.

I have written this healing oracle deck to help you heal your heart and fall in love with yourself. Each card offers you an understanding of what you need to focus on in your journey of heart healing so you can live and love more fully. The more you work with these cards and the heart-healing processes I have shared the more alive, vibrant, inspired, intuitive, passionate, warm, loving and creative you will feel.

Recovering after heartbreak is an individual process that requires great care, wisdom and time. I hope this deck stirs you to be gentle and kind with your heart and to view your painful experiences in a new and empowered way.

These cards will work incredibly well in conjunction with journaling. I hope that as you explore these cards you will be inspired to hear your inner voice and write your own love letters to your heart.

Love and blessings,

INNA SEGAL

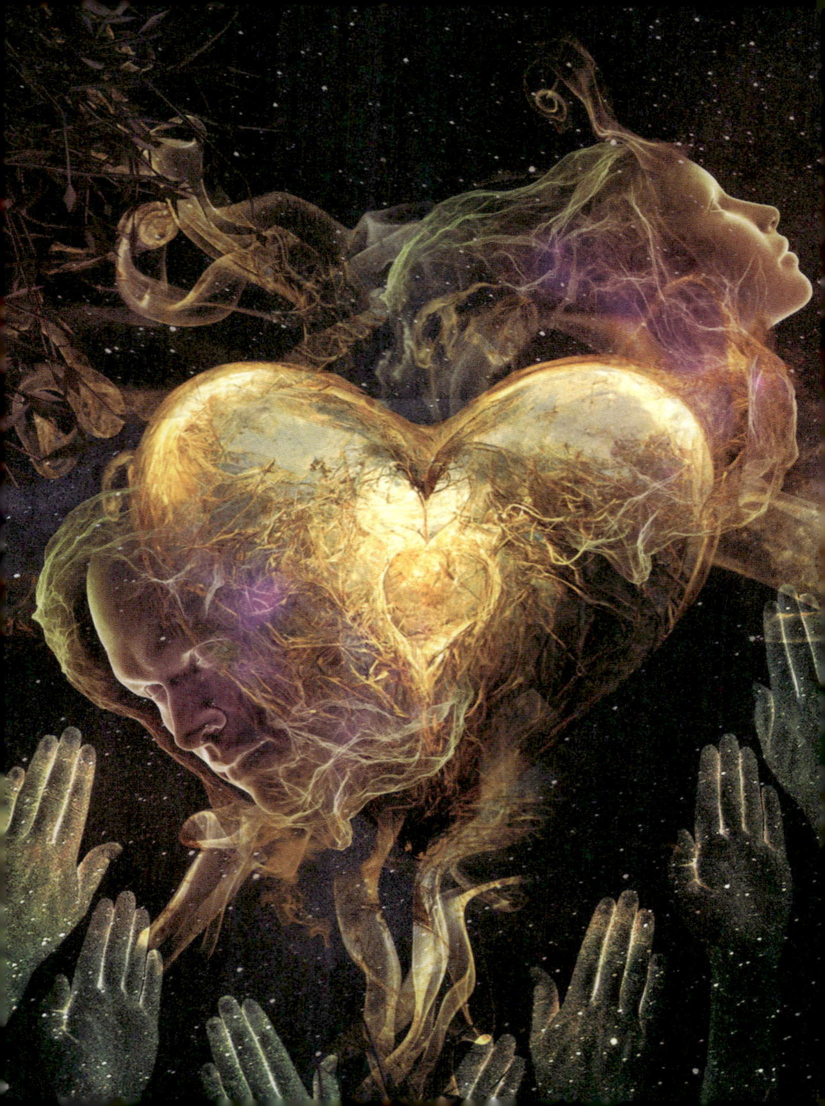

# HOW TO USE THE CARDS

You can receive insights, guidance and messages by placing these cards against your heart and intending to receive. You may feel guided along a new path or be directed to communicate something to your intimate partner, child, family member, work colleague or friend. If you receive a message like this take your time to reflect on what result you would like from your sharing and how it is likely to make your heart feel, then share with them in person or through writing to them.

I encourage you to sit with the image of the card or the cards you pick before reading the guidebook. Every image in this card deck has been meditated over and arose from the deeper wisdom of the heart, so please give yourself an opportunity to feel what each card brings up and allow it to speak to you. In particular, take some time to find the hidden symbols in each image and allow them to reveal a more profound meaning of what the card is about. Contemplate the changes you are being asked to make with an open heart and courage.

I urge you to work with the heart-healing processes connected to the cards you pick for as long it takes to heal.

Whether you pick one card or several, I encourage you to sit with each image and ask yourself the following questions:

- ♥ How does each aspect of this picture make me feel?
- ♥ What connections can I see between the image and what I am feeling in my heart?
- ♥ What is the mood of this card?
- ♥ How do the colours impact me?
- ♥ Which aspect or aspects of the picture awaken something in me and why?
- ♥ What, if any, memories or feelings is this image stirring in me?
- ♥ Can I look at those memories or feelings from a new, more healing perspective?
- ♥ In what way is this card asking me to listen to my heart and take another step forward?

For the best results, work with your cards weekly and commit to the card practice/s for at least seven days. This will give your heart an opportunity to integrate the energies and guidance of your readings, allowing fresh and important insights to awaken.

# ONE-CARD READING

I

Hold the cards and state your intention, such as, 'I ask to receive the clearest, most accurate reading in relation to what is occurring within my heart and the healing steps I need to take.'

Hold the cards to your heart, ask a question and shuffle the cards until you feel guided to stop. Fan the cards across a flat surface or in your hands and pull a single card you feel drawn to. Focus on the card image. Ask yourself the questions listed above, feeling into your heart and allowing insights to surface.

Meditate on how the image makes you feel and how its message relates to what you are feeling in your heart. Focus on all the details in the image: it's often the hidden aspects that awaken the deepest understandings within us. Read the guidebook and complete the practice associated with the card.

The exercises are powerful and can transform your life, so make sure you take the time to do them carefully. I encourage you to do the exercise every day for a week. Have the card near your bed, meditate on it for a few minutes each day and see if any new insights come. Journal those insights, then continue with the process.

# TWO-CARD READING

1    2

Focus on your intention and hold the cards to your heart. Shuffle the cards until you feel guided to stop, then fan them across a flat surface or in your hands. Pull a single card you feel drawn to and contemplate its insights, truly exploring it. Ask yourself: 'What do I need to understand?'

Reshuffle the cards, pick one card and take your time absorbing its wisdom. Ask yourself: 'What do I need to transform?' Complete the card's exercise or practice to integrate its guidance.

# THREE-CARD READING

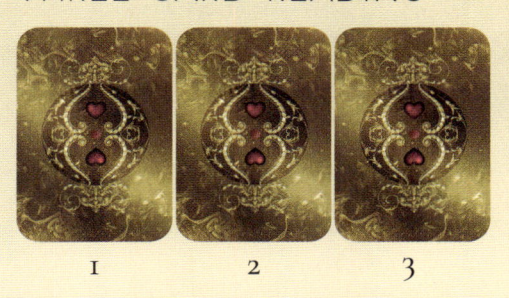

Focus on your intention and shuffle the cards, holding the deck to your heart between each card pull. Ask the following questions before selecting each card:

- ♥ **Card 1:** what have I pushed down or suppressed in my heart?
- ♥ **Card 2:** what aspects of my heart do I need to work on now in order to experience self-love?
- ♥ **Card 3:** what aspect of my heart do I need to heal in order to open my heart to another person?

You can also do an alternative card reading:

- ♥ **Card 1:** what is my biggest emotional challenge right now?
- ♥ **Card 2:** what am I resisting?
- ♥ **Card 3:** what do I need to focus on, amplify or strengthen?

A card drawn upside down indicates a challenge: it is asking you to work with the card to make big life changes. I suggest working with each process for between seven and 30 days.

# FOUR-CARD READING

Shuffle the deck and choose four cards, then consider the following:

- **Card 1:** what was your biggest heart challenge in the past?
- **Card 2:** what is your heart challenge in the present?
- **Card 3:** what do you need to be aware of in the future that could hold you back or move you forward in relationships?
- **Card 4:** the overall message of the reading. Take some time to reflect on how this message is related to the past, the present and the future.

# CHOICE READING

Identify an opportunity in your life that has two or more choices; in particular, relating to relationships or a dream that you would like to manifest. Hold the cards to your heart and hold a choice in your mind as you shuffle the deck and choose three cards:

- ♥ **Card 1:** the emotional challenge or possibility this choice holds.
- ♥ **Card 2:** the lessons or challenges this choice will bring.
- ♥ **Card 3:** the possible outcome of this choice.

Reshuffle the cards and repeat for each choice.

# REPEATED MESSAGES

If you repeatedly choose the same card then you need to read the message several times and take more time to contemplate what the card is asking you as well as work with the process described.

If you already know of other ways to read your cards, feel free to apply those reading methods to this deck.

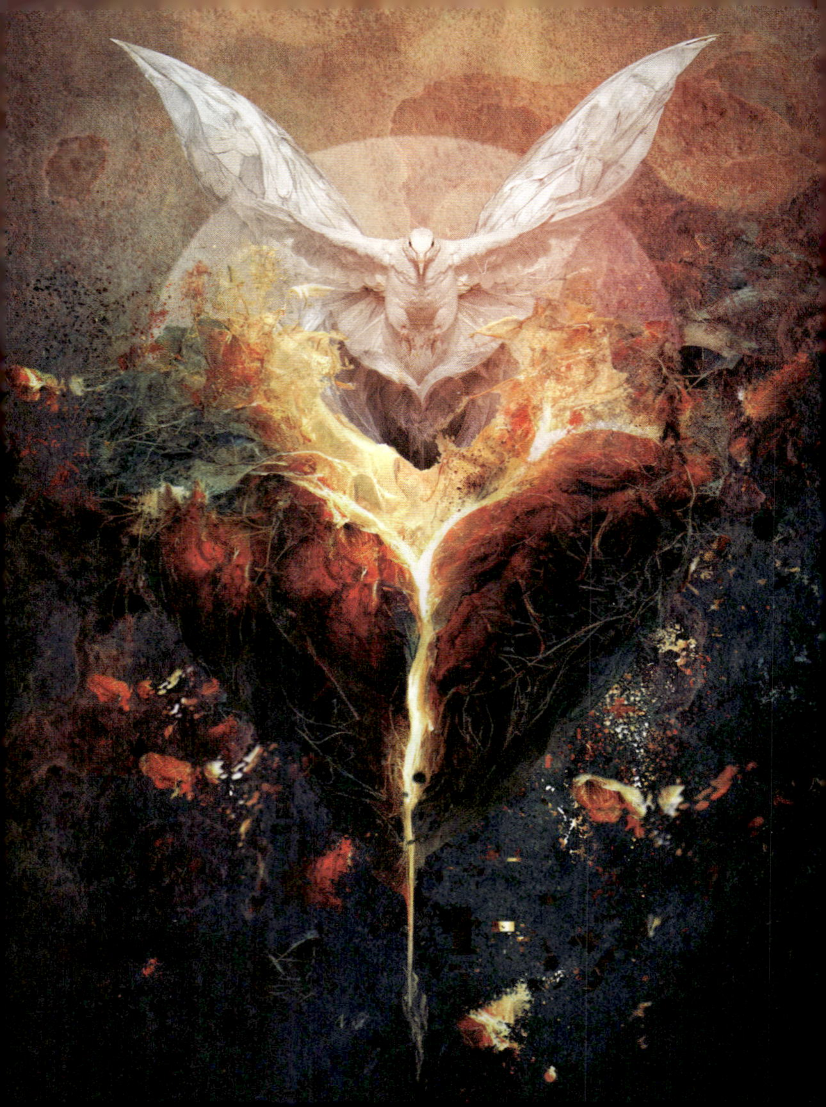

# THE CARDS

# HURT HEART

## I SEE YOU

Dear hurt heart, I know you carry lots of sadness inside you, that it is very easy for you to take things personally and try to self-protect. You feel so scared, little and vulnerable inside that you have needed an armour of spikes to protect you. At times people see you as cold and calculating, but in fact you are so tender and sensitive that if the armour was taken off you could simply bleed out.

I know this is not necessarily how you started but all the rejection, humiliation, neglect and cruelty have deeply wounded you. I see you. I feel your pain is deep. I know there are many cuts and scars all over your heart, and that you have been hurt and you have hurt.

But it is a vicious cycle.

Now is an opportunity to look back on the hurt heart story. It's time to cry the tears that have been frozen and start to bring more light to the buried pain. I promise to start to nourish you with gentle soft caresses, love, kindness and warmth.

## HEART HEALING

Imagine taking out this hurt part of your heart and holding it in your hands. Visualise green healing light and send your heart this green light of healing strength and loving kindness. Speak to your hurt heart and let it know that it can become whole, wise and expanded. Visualise taking out any symbolic spikes representing the hurt it has suffered and place them into an imaginary purple fire with the intention of letting go of old pain, then send your heart emerald-green energy with the intention of rejuvenating it. Place this energetic heart that has received healing energy back into your heart, then take some slow, deep breaths in and out and allow the new healing energy to assimilate. Keep doing this process daily until your heart feels more whole.

# WORTHY HEART

## YOU ARE ENOUGH

Dear heart, I know you carry brokenness, criticism and not feeling good enough within you. You don't believe that you are worthy of comfort, kindness, acknowledgement and encouragement. You hide, because you are unsure of yourself, your talents, abilities and most of all your value in intimate relationships.

I feel you, because you are not alone. Like many other hearts, you bought into the story of lack. You have been so busy looking outside for love and acknowledgement that you have forgotten how to refill your own inner cup.

Deep inside you know that no matter how much others say they like you or love you, and unless you can practise self-love you will always feel like you're not enough. The truth is that you are enough; you are more than enough! You are bountiful, you are beautiful and you are divine.

---

## HEART HEALING

Tune in to this part of your heart and ask: 'What do you require to become full?' Allow an answer to arise as a thought or feeling, then record it in a journal or draw a picture of what you feel this aspect needs to expand and strengthen.

Make time to caress this heart. Tell it words of encouragement and visualise peach rays of light filling it up with the most incredible sense of self-worth, belief and vitality. Cherish this heart.

# UNSEEN HEART

## YOU ARE SIGNIFICANT

Dear heart, I know the pain you have been through of feeling ignored, discounted and brushed off. There is never enough time in a day, week, month or year to give you the care and the attention you crave. You, darling heart, have been so patient, tolerant, understanding, compromising and forgiving. You wait for a time when you can be given consideration, kindness and most of all thoughtfulness.

You need to feel that you matter, that you are precious and significant. At times you don't know how to respond to all the past coldness you have encountered, and it can be particularly painful to have your feelings, ideas and intuition discounted. There are parts of yourself that you don't even know anymore, as they have become so rigid, stunted and weary.

I am here for you, dear unseen heart. I am ready to see, love, accept and embrace all of you. To me every part of you is important, interesting and precious. I now take full responsibility for you and I give you permission to grow into the huge heart that you are. Together we will bring goodness and beauty to others. Together we will see those who have been hiding for eternity and we will help them cultivate their divinity.

## HEART HEALING

Close your eyes and take slow deep breaths in and out. Find the aspect of your heart that has been unseen by you and others: what does this part of your heart look like? Does it resemble a tiny speck of dust, a scared child or a black caterpillar that has never bloomed into a butterfly? What thoughts, feelings and experiences are held in this unheeded heart? Can you take some time to see, accept and love what has previously been in hiding?

# REBELLIOUS HEART

## THINK FOR YOURSELF

Dear heart, you have rebelled against rules, conditioning and indoctrination. You have withstood storms and danced with chaos and have had the courage to think for yourself even when your beliefs or ideas were unpopular.

There have been moments when you have been wild and untamed and tried things that blew up in your face, but at least you did something different. You didn't conform to the norm and thus you allowed the creative, adventurous you to grow. You have made mistakes and at times ignored the voice of reason and for that you have suffered and struggled, but even during the dark night of the soul you never, ever gave up.

When I think about the battles you have fought and won you give me strength to keep moving forward, growing and evolving. I want us to work together and keep becoming wiser, my daring heart. I no longer want to jump into situations that have the potential to crush us without thinking about the consequences first. At the same time I never want you to conform to other people's ways of thinking and living their lives.

## HEART HEALING

Close your eyes and take some deep breaths in and out. If this heart had a form, what would it look like: would it be healthy or unhealthy? What is your true relationship with your rebellious heart: are you letting it dominate your life or suppressing it, or is it a healthy part of you that appears when you need it?

Take some time to discover the true gift of the rebellious heart by inviting it to offer you new and interesting possibilities that contain shrewdness within them.

## 05

# TRUSTING HEART

### LISTEN TO YOUR INNER WISDOM

Dear heart, I know you desire to trust others fully. You want to believe that everyone connects to you from a place of purity and goodness. When you open you shine and attract others to you. You let them into your inner garden, a place that is sacred and delicate. This place contains many colours and feelings.

The more you allow, the more the colours get brighter and the feelings grow stronger. When you trust and love you fill your soul and body with wonderful revitalising energy. This experience is sublime and makes you feel connected to all of humanity and divinity. At times you may even forget that each person holds both shadow and light aspects. You may ignore that people can be tempted by greed, selfishness and power. When people – including you, my dear heart – become self-focused they can hurt and crush others.

You may have experienced the devastating pain of betrayal from a lover, a friend, a work colleague or even a close family member. It may have stung so badly that you shut your heart and barricaded it with the hardiest planks you could master.

What if trust is something you could develop by connecting with and listening to the wisdom of your experiences? Maybe you no longer need to give yourself away to a person who cannot love, honour and cherish you. What if you could start to trust your courage to get up whenever you've been knocked down?

## HEART HEALING

Close your eyes and focus on the wisest part of your heart. If it was a person, what would she or he look like? Ask this wise you to share with the younger, more trusting hurt you what it needs to hear, then imagine the wise heart holding any broken pieces of the trusting heart and healing them. Observe as the wise you places this more whole heart into your chest. Thank the wiser you and allow it to merge inside your inner being, knowing that no matter what happens you have the strength to get back up.

# KNOWING HEART
## HEED YOUR INTUITION

Dear heart, you have lived with immense pressure to always know what to do in any given circumstance, yet even you, my knowing heart, can become tired, numb, hurt and confused if you are not supported. You may even buckle under the stress of having to make huge decisions, which will impact every part of my life.

I often implore you to know all the answers without giving you the rest and the nourishment you need. I beseech you to tell me about my love life without helping you heal from past hurts, yet when you warn me that there could be likelihood of a lot of pain I turn away from you and ignore you. I then act on my desires and become crushed when things don't work out, saying that your warning was not loud enough. I expect you to step up and have a sharp intuition without realising that if I keep ignoring your whispers they get softer.

I'm sorry for the intensity of my expectations. I know I need to listen more and recognise that at times you need healing, kindness and fun to recover in order to be able to offer the best of yourself. I am willing to slow down, connect with you and heed your intuition.

## HEART HEALING

Close your eyes and ask to meet your knowing heart. If this part had a face what would it look like: does it seem happy, tense or sad? Does this part of you need any regeneration, love and compassion? How can you offer this: is it through loving words, rest, kind actions and a gentle touch? Take a moment to do whatever feels right.

If the knowing heart had a voice, what would it say to you right now? Listen. Thank this part and start heeding it.

## 07

# CURIOUS HEART

### EMBARK ON A GREAT ADVENTURE

Dear heart, I absolutely adore when you show your cheeky, curious spirit. I love your desire to learn, discover and co-create. I know that whenever you encounter something that inspires you, you swell up with joy, colour and juiciness. You encourage me to try new things, guide me forward and challenge me to become more daring, and when I listen I become light, energised and full of aliveness. I know

I feel incredible when we are truly connected, yet I tend to ignore you, become over serious and sweat the small stuff.

I'm sorry for neglecting you and making you feel like everything else is more important than exploring and learning. I now know that curiosity can lead me to the discovery of my own unique nature and the most thrilling adventures. Dear heart, please open yourself to me so that we can embark on our greatest adventure.

---

## HEART HEALING

Where in your being does the curious heart hide? Encourage this part of you to emerge in all its colourful glory. Place your hands on your heart and ask: 'What am I curious about now? What am I ready to explore?' Give yourself permission to be daring and discover what is the most meaningful to you right now.

Do something interesting and fun towards this exploration in the next 48 hours. If doubts arise, then doubt the doubt!

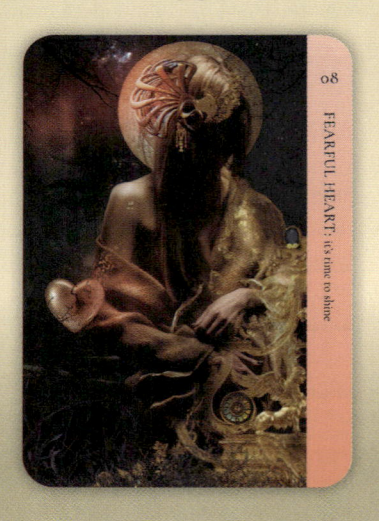

# FEARFUL HEART

## IT'S TIME TO SHINE

Dear heart, I know you feel small and afraid. You have suffered the consequences of being belittled and hurt, which has made you want to hide and become invisible to others. You have given more attention to why something may not work as opposed to why it could. You have experienced heartbreak and heartache many a time.

    I feel you. You are tired, lonely and self-protective. It has been easy for you to sabotage everything from intimate connections to great career opportunities. I am ready to embrace you and allow you to grow so you can start to recognise your true worth and power.

Fear has made you see only one side of the story. It is time to explore your journey from a space of courage and strength and it is time for you to shine, my sweet, fragile heart.

## HEART HEALING

Imagine what a fearful heart would look like: would it be dark, small and gooey? Visualise holding it in the palm of your hand. With the other hand, caress this anxious heart while encouraging it to strengthen and become courageous. Truly see how much this aspect has suffered and lovingly embrace it. Energetically place it back into your heart and make a decision to do something courageous within the next 72 hours, then take action.

## 09

# DEEP HEART

## BELIEVE IN DIVINE DESTINY

Dear heart, at times you feel so alone as you don't think you can find the people who can truly see, hear and understand you. This can cause you to despair and shut down or put on a mask so that you can feel that you belong. You are sensitive and intuitive, yet people can see you as hardened.

There is so much you want to share with others but you simply don't know where to turn or who to pour your heart out to. I want to reassure you that if you choose to trust and show some vulnerability you will find those who truly appreciate you for all that you are.

The time has come to make a choice to fully get to know yourself and believe in your divine destiny. You can lament about the past all you like and get stuck in a rut, or you can dare to dream and follow your soul's calling and move forward with confidence. I am ready to embrace you for all that you are.

---

## HEART HEALING

Place your hands on your heart and feel its depth. Tune in to what your heart needs to grow, evolve and feel fuller. Imagine offering this to your heart: how does it feel? Visualise yourself exploring a deeper connection with your heart and soul and taking steps towards living the type of life that makes your inner life and your heart blossom.

## 10.

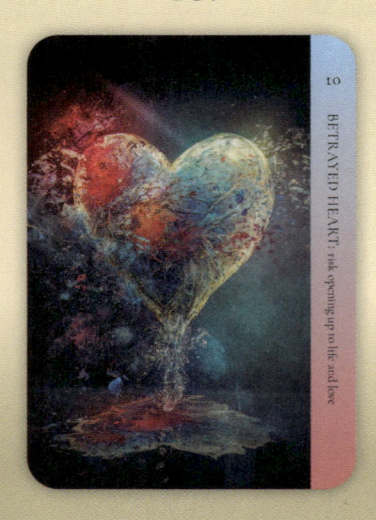

# BETRAYED HEART

### RISK OPENING UP TO LIFE AND LOVE

Dear heart, I know that you can be incredibly loving, soft and giving. Now and then you put your trust into those who you care about implicitly even when there are signs to the contrary. You forgive their hurtful deeds and unkind words and occasionally even turn a blind eye to their untruthfulness. At times you get caught so unaware by the harmful and even cruel actions of those you love that you erupt or even shatter into small pieces.

I know how deeply deceit and betrayal can sting, dear heart. It can literally bring you to your knees and stop you from trusting, opening or growing. It can cut you off from joy and even your spirit nature. Betrayal can either crush you or it can allow you to learn, mature and flourish.

The time has come when you must decide in which direction you want to go. Do you want to hide, protect and limit or are you ready to be courageous and risk opening yourself to new aspects of life and love, even if it's not easy?

## HEART HEALING

Close your eyes and place your hand on your heart. Feel into the part of your heart that has been deceived or betrayed and sense if there are pieces that have been cracked or broken. If there are, imagine taking them out with your right hand and placing them into the palm of your left hand. Visualise soft green light coming out of the fingers of your right hand. Caress these shattered pieces of your heart and communicate with them in loving words, encouraging healing, strength and courage.

Observe as these fractured pieces repair and transform, then energetically place them back into your heart. Place your hands on your heart and focus on all the positives that have come out of your painful experiences.

## II.

# CO-CREATIVE HEART
## LOOK FOR CLEAR SIGNS

Dear heart, I know that when I listen to your whispers and hear your inner call we become an incredible team for manifesting the type of reality and life we both desire. I know that I can easily forget to align with you: I become so busy that instead of tuning in to you I go to a place of safety in my head. I try to be practical and realistic as opposed to following my passion, creativity and joy.

I know that you hold the key to my destiny and that I need to reconnect with you by asking the right questions: 'What makes you open, my dear heart? What makes you come alive and experience happiness, joy and fulfilment? What gives you a sense of wholeness and satisfaction? What is your true calling?'

I am willing to be patient and meditate on these questions, and pay attention to the feelings I receive and the answers you offer me. I ask that you make the answers clear, including offering me strong signs that I can recognise and follow.

## HEART HEALING

Place your hands on your heart and allow yourself to feel into your heart: does it feel empty or full? If it is empty ask: 'What can I do to bring more satisfaction and enthusiasm into my heart?'

Decide to take some action towards doing heart-felt activities. Meditate on the questions above to allow your heart to open and guide you towards fulfilling your destiny and loving your life experience. Visualise what you really desire and imagine completely receiving it with every part of your heart. Know that good things are coming towards you.

# 12.

# RESILIENT HEART

## IT'S TIME TO REBUILD

Dear heart, today I ask you to forgive me for all the times I didn't listen to you. I know that by ignoring your counsel I put you through heartbreak, pain, distress, confusion and suffering. There have been moments when you felt shattered, and instead of supporting you I neglected you and tried everything I could to distract and distance myself from your pain.

I know you have felt incredibly lonely and at times rejected and unwanted. You have often wondered what is wrong with you, why you are so different and whether anyone will ever see you for all that you are, yet through all the isolation, hurt, betrayal and abandonment you still had faith that I would come back to you and that we would rebuild a healthy relationship, a connection that is based on self-love, inner security, acceptance, nourishment and care.

I thank you deeply for being so strong, patient and available to lead me towards experiencing profound love and destiny as well as emotional and spiritual growth. I am now willing to heed your wisdom and embrace your intuitive guidance.

---

# HEART HEALING

Rub your hands together then put them slightly apart. Imagine a warm, sunlit, yellow energy coming out of the palms of your hands and focus on sending appreciation, recognition and gratitude for all that your heart and you have been through. Place your hands on your heart and breathe the warm, yellow light into the depth of your heart. If you had loving words to say to your heart what would they be? Say them to yourself or out aloud.

Give yourself permission to connect with, ask questions of and be guided by the wisdom of your heart in all aspects of your life.

## 13.

# GRIEVING HEART

### OPEN DOORS TO SOMETHING NEW

Dear grieving heart, I know you feel disoriented and confused. Losing those we love and are close to is always difficult, and you may be experiencing fear, hurt and apprehension about the future. Your sense of self may have diminished as you have had thoughts such as 'I don't know who I am, and I no longer know what I love, what I care about or what makes me sing.' You might feel numb or anxious and not want to participate in everyday life.

Dear heart, it is important that you give yourself time to mourn your loss and heal. You also must gain the wisdom that this difficult experience has brought you. Embracing the opportunity to become more independent, shrewd and clear can feel uncomfortable but it can offer you incredible growth and self-confidence.

Take some time to reflect on what you have truly lost: is it love, friendship, understanding, help or care? Reflect on how this loss can open doors to something new.

---

# HEART HEALING

Record on paper everything you gained from what you went through with a particular person, animal, job or experience. What were the truly inspiring aspects that made your soul shine? Acknowledge those. Record what you feel you lost by having this person, animal, job or experience leave your life. It could be anything from no longer having free time for yourself to losing your sense of self or giving too much of yourself away. Be super honest with yourself.

Complete the healing by writing down what is possible for you to explore in your life without this person, pet, job or experience that could help you heal, revitalise and expand.

## 14.

# GIVING HEART

## DEVELOP SELF-LOVE

Dear heart, I love your generosity, benevolence and thoughtfulness. I know how much you adore giving of yourself to others, as you genuinely believe that the more you give the more you will receive. However, at times it can become overwhelming to share so much of yourself, especially when others choose to take advantage of you rather than exchange with you. It may even feel as though you are literally giving yourself away.

You also have a tendency to trust those who are struggling, failing or self-sabotaging. Your tenderness, kindness, honesty and sensitivity are beautiful but it is vital that you start to establish some healthy boundaries. It's time to use your life experience to discern those who truly need your help and will appreciate it from those who just want to use you.

Give yourself permission to renourish and love yourself. Make time for fun, laughter and healing. Recognise and reward yourself regularly and your confidence will grow, which will allow you to receive all the creativity, affection, abundance and juiciness that you deserve so that you can give from a place of fullness.

## HEART HEALING

Find a day, half a day or even a few hours to take yourself on a renourishing date. Do something on your own that revitalises your heart and soul and is soothing to your feelings. This could be as simple as going for a walk in the park or on the beach, or you could have a relaxing bubble bath while listening to gentle music. Maybe taking some time to rest and meditate is what your inner being needs or, on the other hand, having a relaxing massage or facial or taking yourself out for a delicious lunch might hit the spot.

Whatever it is, make sure that you start giving back to your heart and engaging your creative, warm, intuitive, passionate self.

## 15.

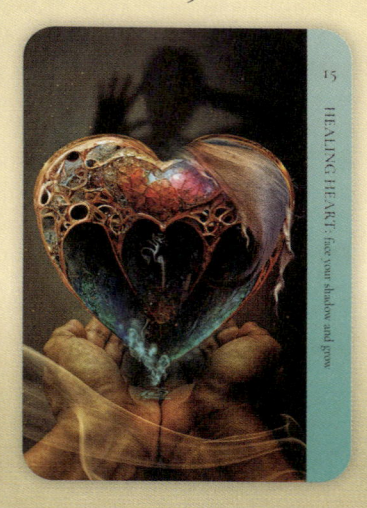

# HEALING HEART

## FACE YOUR SHADOW AND GROW

Dear heart, I know you have experienced neglect, rejection, disappointment and betrayal from those you loved and cared about. This has hurt you deeply and made aspects of your inner self shut down or even wilt away. On some level you are still holding on to old trauma, whether it was abuse from your childhood, humiliation or disloyalty from someone you loved, cruelty from those you trusted or a failure in a relationship or business.

Over time old wounds that have not been lovingly met and healed can fester and sabotage your future. Rather than being open to love you can shut out those who could appreciate, cherish and encourage you. Unhealed pain can also inhibit you from listening to your intuition and daring to follow your dreams.

The time has come to face your shadow and heal your trauma so you can expand and grow. We can then partner up, dear heart, and discern what will strengthen us and where to put our love, care, energy and attention.

## HEART HEALING

Place your hands on your heart. If the hurt part had a face and a body, what would it look like? Give this archetype permission to share what it feels and what trauma it is still carrying. Really listen. Imagine a purple flame in front of you, and with your hands help this part release anything that it is ready to let go of into the fire. Hold this aspect close to you and say: 'Dear [give this aspect a name], you are loved, seen, heard and supported. Together we will now reclaim your power and an ability to grow and heal.'

Allow this part of you to receive this message. If you need to, add anything else and then imagine that this part reassimilates into your heart in a healthier way, allowing your heart to heal. Keep doing this process daily until you experience deeper healing.

## 16.

# PASSIONATE HEART

## USE YOUR VOICE TO WAKE UP OTHERS

Dear heart, I know you have a deep desire to help others and see those you love succeed. You also want the world to be full of kind souls who harbour positive intentions to create love, harmony and peace. You crave residing in a society where people are supported to live healthier, more dignified lives. At times you witness major injustices and contradictory behaviours from those who are in power and are meant to be examples of honourable leadership. This can bring up anger, frustration and at times even rage at the unfairness and ugliness that confronts you.

If you focus on all that is wrong you will start to feel hopeless and implode. Inside you know you have an opportunity to turn your anger into passion and use it to encourage change. This change can be made through education, fresh perspectives and offering people new opportunities to co-create the kind of world they would love to live in! The idea is to transform frustration into something creative that can inspire others and move society into a healthier direction.

The time has come for you to courageously stand up for what you believe and use your voice and ingenuity to wake people up to what is possible.

## HEART HEALING

Record what makes you feel angry and read over it. If you don't like to write, express your feelings through art, movement or singing. Place your hand on your heart and ask yourself if you can do something to make the situation better. For instance, can you educate others to take positive actions? Can you find or build a community of like-minded people? Can you get out of your comfort zone and do something that will wake up others? Record what you are enthusiastic about and the three immediate steps you can take to turn anger into passion.

## 17.

# TRAPPED HEART

## STEP OUTSIDE YOUR COMFORT ZONE

Dear heart, I know you feel trapped and confused as you are not sure of whom to turn to for help or in what direction to proceed. At times it may appear as though no matter what you do someone seems upset or disappointed.

Inside you may suffer with uncertainty and experience heavy, suffocating emotions. You may even feel like pushing it all down and numbing yourself; after all, you have done that before. However, there is a wiser part of you that says 'Please, please, breathe and feel.'

While it would be easy to continuously occupy yourself, you are being asked to sit quietly with your feelings and allow them to reveal to you what you need to do in order to create more freedom. This could be extremely uncomfortable, as you may need to leave a toxic relationship, change your career, work on transforming old habits, move to a new area or take responsibility for your finances. Whatever it is, you have to face the truth of your situation and gain the courage to step outside your comfort zone, as it is only there that you will find yourself and the freedom of choice you seek.

---

## HEART HEALING

Grab your journal and record the situation you find yourself in. Start to explore whether or not you can see any aspects of what you want to run away from or resist being mirrored to you from the other person or people. If so, are you willing to take responsibility and adjust? Are you being treated harshly by others and not heard? How do you treat yourself? Are you really trapped in a situation, or have you convinced yourself that there is no way out? If there was a way that allowed you to move towards self-love, freedom and healing, what would it be?

Give yourself time to meditate on what that may look like and what preparation you may need to do in order to move forward.

# 18.

# ADVENTUROUS HEART

## SET SAIL ON A TRIP OF A LIFETIME

Dear heart, I know how much you love adventure, excitement and discovering new places, cultures and lifestyles. Every time you go on a trip you come back wiser, deeper and fuller. Each person you meet allows you to view life in a new and more profound manner. I love how whenever you venture out you also go on a journey of self-discovery. You reconnect with the colourful, creative parts of yourself that have previously been asleep or hidden and you allow them to grow and evolve.

The time has come for you to go on another quest, a trip that needs to be meaningfully guided by your intuition. The next step of your destiny awaits you. Give yourself permission to discover more about your soul, love and life: no more sitting around feeling sorry for yourself or sabotaging your opportunities. The time has come for you to courageously plan a trip of a lifetime.

---

## HEART HEALING

Place your hands on your heart and ask where you need to go in order to renourish your creative self. It could be somewhere you have never been in your city or country, or you may decide to travel to another side of the world. Once you have chosen the destination, jump into your car or get on a plane, boat or train and allow yourself to investigate. On the other hand, you might decide that you need to go on the most profound inner journey and discover the depth of your soul and spirituality.

Whatever it is, make sure you give yourself the opportunity and time to explore deeply.

## 19.

# BEAUTIFUL HEART

### OPEN YOUR WINGS AND FLY

Dear heart, I love to see you shine and express all your inner riches. Your beauty exudes warmth, kindness and purity, and your connection to divinity is at its highest when you allow yourself to sparkle. Everyone is attracted to you and wants to be around you to taste the lusciousness of your wisdom. Your softness can feel like a supple pillow where others can land. Your voice exudes the sound of angels and your caress can heal the deepest wounds.

As you allow yourself to taste true love, your wings open to fly high as well as be of comfort and support to all who need your affection and care. No more hiding, my beautiful, courageous, potent, tender heart. It is time for you to shimmer with all your colourful, creative, unique flair!

## HEART HEALING

Place your hands on your heart and give yourself permission to express all that is beautiful within you. For the next week, wherever you go look for what is lovely, healing, wonderful, spectacular, exquisite and impressively beautiful. This can be an inner quality in a person or it could be a work of art that you acknowledge.

Allow yourself to bask in the magnificence of life and all that you recognise. Each day, record in your journal five beautiful qualities you have exhibited that day, then take a few moments to meditate on the positive feelings and the heart opening that occurs within you.

## 20.

# DON'T GIVE UP ON LOVE HEART

## WHAT DO YOU DESIRE?

Dear heart, I know you have experienced immense pain and heartbreak. You have gone into survival mode, numbing and pushing away all hurtful feelings while at the same time repressing joy, intuition and love. You have developed immense fear of opening yourself to loving, passionate, giving, connected, empowering and healing relationships.

The time has come for you to gain more inner strength and courage and take a step forward towards love. Know that no matter how much you have tried to convince yourself that love is unattainable, this is not the truth. In fact, there is a magnificent soul that is yearning to connect with you and share your life journey; however, they can only connect with you if you let go of your limited ways of thinking.

If you are already in a relationship, this is a nudge for you to work on letting go of the past and open your heart to a renewed depth of love. If that is not possible with your current partner, then know that there is someone else there for you who can offer you the type of nourishing love you are searching for – but you have to create space for them.

## HEART HEALING

It is time to go beyond your fear and make a commitment to release what is holding you back from meeting the love of your life. Journal what you are afraid of and what you are ready to let go of, then record the qualities you are looking for in an incredible partner. Imagine what this person's energy may feel like and practise opening your heart daily to receiving this person into your life. Dress up and go out to a variety of events where you can meet your dream lover.

If you are in a relationship, give yourself an opportunity to reconnect with your partner and rediscover them and your relationship.

## 21.

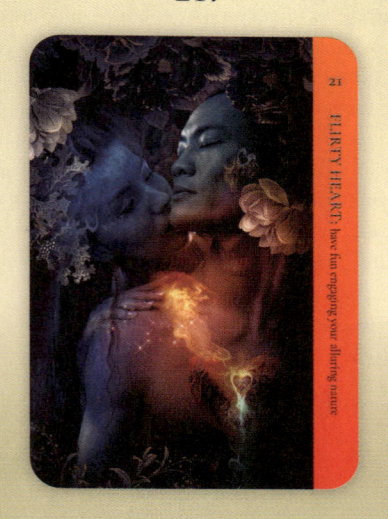

# FLIRTY HEART

## HAVE FUN ENGAGING YOUR ALLURING NATURE

Dear heart, I know how much you love to play, flirt and have fun. You adore expressing your hidden flavours and entertaining those whom you find interesting. You love uncovering the juicy, secret, spicy places within your lover's or a potential admirer's heart.

When you open the gates to love your inner self beautifies and swells with the warmest, sweetest sentiments. Seductive aspects that were previously asleep awaken and aliveness pulses through your veins. You want to be seen, felt, known and adored. Affection drips out of your core and a scent of possibilities orbits your aura. The mystery of your inner riches hangs in the air awaiting your next move.

How fun is it to play and engage your alluring nature, yet so often this part, which can captivate so many, gets hidden or turns brazen. I am ready, dear heart, for you to reveal to me your feminine and masculine charms, helping me to intrigue and titillate all those who appear in my romantic rendezvous.

## HEART HEALING

Place your right hand on your heart and your left hand on your root chakra. Do your heart and sensuality align with each other? Are you open to exploring this part in an honouring, sacred way?

If you have a partner, decide to play a sensual game. You may like to place some candles around, put on romantic music, ask some tantalising questions, give each other a pleasurable massage, dance seductively for each other, have a relaxing bath, do some role playing and really engage in your delicious connection. If you don't have a partner, ask yourself how to flirt and exhibit the light, fun, fetching, engaging part of yourself. How can you move, drink, eat and speak to bring more of your sensual aspects out? Allow yourself to connect to this luscious, yummy energy and express it.

## 22.

# CAUTIOUS HEART
### HAVE ENOUGH WISDOM TO GET BACK UP

Dear heart, I know you have experienced some painful losses and this has made you cautious. You are wary of anyone new coming close and creating havoc inside your inner being. You have shut down your deepest feelings and have resorted to being a watchdog for potential danger. You have experienced so much disappointment in your earlier life that you no longer allow space for spontaneity. Your soft, intuitive, freedom loving self has been squeezed out to make room for control, tension and shells of protection.

The time has come, dear heart, for you to step out of fear and into trust. This is not about trusting someone else but about having the faith: that if you fall or have a setback in your life or your relationships you have now developed enough wisdom and strength to get back up. This is not about doing something extreme but about slowly and gently opening yourself up to life's wonders.

## HEART HEALING

Close your eyes and place your hands on your heart. Ask your heart what you are afraid of. Allow it to share with you any feelings, images or thoughts related to what it is holding on to. If you have a journal, record any insights and what you have learned from each difficult experience.

Allow the wisdom from your learning to strengthen your heart and offer you the capacity to move forward with the awareness that you can now see the potential challenges as well as the possible successes in each opportunity.

## 23.

# PATIENT HEART

### MOVE FORWARD AND GROW

Dear heart, thank you for being incredibly patient with all my toing and froing. It can be extremely difficult for me to make up my mind about a particular situation or a person. Sometimes I feel as though I have one foot out moving towards my dreams and the other foot on a break, trying to protect myself from a potential disaster.

I know that I have not always made the best decisions and you have taken some big emotional hits, yet you still wait patiently for me to self-reflect and learn from my faux pas. You are constantly reminding me that there are new adventures ahead of me that can bring me great joy. You use your feelings to point me in a direction where I can gather great insights, but even when I have an opportunity to learn and grow I sometimes resist with all my might.

I am grateful to you, my dear heart, that you have not forsaken me and still hold space for me to receive divine love, self-love and human love. I am on my way.

## HEART HEALING

Take a few moments to reflect on how patient your heart has been with you in terms of love, discovering your purpose and your inner growth. Place your hand on your heart and truly thank it for being so enduring and persistent.

Reflect on an important relationship in your life with a partner, child, family member, work colleague or friend: is there a person in your life at present who requires you to be patient, kind and loving with them? If there is, make a conscious effort to encourage them gently while acknowledging where they are at in life. Show them the kindness they need at present.

# HUNGRY HEART

## AWAKEN THE TRUE SONG OF YOUR HEART

Dear heart, I know you hunger for the most profound depth, intensity, passion, juiciness and divine ecstasy. You want to taste and embody all that love entails, and you desire to feel all your layers of protection melt and to be truly seen and held by another. You want to be appreciated for all of you, the beautiful and the painful. You want someone to support you through your unprocessed trauma with gentle kindness and compassion.

All of this is possible, my darling heart. You have been starved of genuine affection, kindness and gentleness, and I am now ready to truly see, listen and treat you with outmost respect and kindness so you can heal. I want to help you awaken the true song of your heart and your ability to befriend and learn from all your feelings. This will create a wholeness and stability within your being where you can develop concentration, self-reflection, steadfastness and an intimate self-knowingness.

## HEART HEALING

Take five minutes each morning for the next 30 days to connect with your heart and ask what aspects of your inner self you need to awaken or transform. Allow an answer to come then say: 'I hear you!' Take a few deep breaths and reflect on what you are really hearing then tell your heart: 'I see you!' Make sure you repeat this several times, then proceed to follow your heart's deeper guidance on a daily basis.

# REMORSEFUL HEART

## FORGIVE AND MOVE AHEAD

Dear heart, I know you have made some questionable choices and injured other souls. At times we all need to reflect on our thoughtless, impulsive, insensitive behaviour.

The remorse you are feeling can be of great use for your future development if you can genuinely learn from your past experience and make a choice to act in a benevolent way. If it is a particular person you have hurt with your callous words and actions, take an opportunity to express your new understanding and genuinely ask for forgiveness when it is appropriate. If that is not possible in person then do so in your imagination. Their soul will hear you even if they are on the other side of the planet or no longer reside on earth.

If, on the other hand, you decide to push your guilt down you are likely to end up with a variety of unpleasant ailments. At times forgiveness may not be directed to another but to yourself in order to let go of the old and open the door for the future.

## HEART HEALING

Close your eyes and place your hands on the part of your body where you feel remorse. Imagine the person you have hurt standing in front of you and vulnerably express to them any profound realisations you have acquired about what had occurred. Thank them for listening and ask them to respond from their heart. Allow yourself to receive healing energy from this exchange.

If this person is alive and can be reached, try to connect with them and share your feelings in person or send them a handwritten letter from your heart.

## 26.

# RECOVERING HEART

## STEP ONTO THE ROAD TO DEEPER HEALING

Dear heart, I know you have been through much struggle, grief and brokenness. In many ways life has not turned out the way you dreamed and I am sure that at times you have wondered what you have done wrong to deserve the torment you have encountered. Some of your injuries have been so immense you probably never thought you would be able to recover.

At times you still hold your breath and struggle to get through the day without falling apart, yet after all the loss, grief and suffering you are still standing, my dear heart. In fact, while something deep inside you may have shattered, something new and more pure has also been born. You have become deeper, stronger and more conscious of what is truly valuable in life.

Your ability to have compassion, express kindness and patience and take the higher road has amplified dramatically. You are not only on the road to healing but to also knowing who you truly are and have the capacity to become.

## HEART HEALING

Place your hands on your heart and take some deep breaths in and out. From the depth of your soul, acknowledge what you have been through and reflect on where you are at now in your healing journey. Give yourself some credit for how far you have come. Ask your heart what it needs in order to continue reviving, then make a list of the steps you can take on a daily basis to help fill your heart's cup.

# 27.

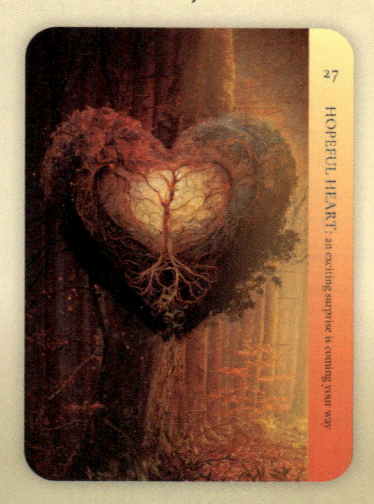

# HOPEFUL HEART

## AN EXCITING SURPRISE IS COMING YOUR WAY

Dear heart, your journey towards healing, trust and openness has been an arduous one. It is important you don't lose hope and that you keep taking courageous steps forward and learning more about yourself in various life situations.

No matter what you might be feeling at the moment, there is an exciting surprise coming your way. It is something you have been requesting for a long time, so keep your inner door open and take some risks as this has a high likelihood of turning out very fruitfully for you. However, you must meet your fear of loss and transform it into an openness to receive what you desire. It is time to start to value yourself and develop self-love.

Remember you have been though a lot and have learned a great deal, so you deserve all the joy and happiness that is coming your way.

## HEART HEALING

The time has come to allow yourself to dream again. Record in your journal any dreams or heart desires you have. Read over each of them and ask: 'Is there anything that I am afraid of that stops me moving forward?' If there is, take slow, deep breaths in and out and ask what would happen if you could face this fear. Allow an answer to arise. Make a decision to start living your life fully and take some risks in the areas of life and love.

## 28.

# DARING HEART

## LEARN TO LEAD FROM WISDOM

Dear heart, I love your daring nature and willingness to explore beyond the norm. You have a tendency to push the limits of love and fate and your desire to live every moment to the fullest is exhilarating. Your valour and leadership qualities are going to be greatly necessary in the imminent future.

It is important that you give yourself time to relax, strengthen and recover as you are about to enter a battlefield. You will be required to lead from wisdom instead of pure emotion or passion. All the skills you have learned in the past now need to be refined in order to be utilised in the most effective manner.

You are a sage in the making, so if you slow down and listen to your intuition in what is about to ensue the results will be rewarding, but if you ignore your insight then disaster will arise.

## HEART HEALING

The time has come to do something daring while still listening to the wisdom of your heart. What project have you been itching to start or become a part of? What have you been holding back on and allowing your fear to rule? Is there something you need to express to someone? Is there a discovery trip you need to go on? Is there something you need to give up that no longer serves you? Whatever it is, find the inner courage within you to start thriving.

## 29.

# PROSPERING HEART

## LOOK FOR BEAUTY, ABUNDANCE AND GENEROSITY

Dear heart, you have spent a lot of time limiting, struggling, pushing and playing small. This has left you exhausted and living in a state of inner tension and survival.

The tide is changing and you must consciously transform your focus from looking at limitations, weakness and suffering to seeing the beauty, abundance and generosity in the world. Stop complaining that there is not enough love, kindness, depth, care, ethics, help and abundance and start looking at the world with new eyes and singing a different tune. The most fantastic, abundant opportunities of your life are waiting for you to get ready to receive. They are coming to you from the divine source itself and will appear at the perfect time.

---

## HEART HEALING

This is not the time to sit and wait. Get clear on what it is you are ready to receive and create a vision board. Every morning and evening say: 'If it is for my highest good then I ask that divine intelligence brings [state what it is] into my life in perfect time and in perfect ways with ease and grace.'

Really focus on embracing what is for your highest good then state: 'I choose to allow prosperity to flow to me from the divine source itself. All that is mine by divine design now reaches me in great avalanches of abundance under grace in miraculous ways.' Close your eyes and imagine receiving what you desire with ease and grace.

# REINVENTING HEART

## GET TO KNOW YOURSELF ANEW

Dear heart, you have gone through a period of stagnation and feeling flat. It is time to get out of your usual routine and any slump you have been in and become creative.

You have an opportunity to get to know yourself anew at this particular stage of life. Things are changing and it is time to reinvent yourself, which could mean looking within and meeting any aspects of yourself you have pushed away or disowned or going on an adventure that involves self-discovery.

It's time to let go of any old and dreary energy, step out of your comfort zone and embrace your vibrant, delicious, surprising colours! Say 'Yes' to exploring any new and exciting ventures, as you will be delighted with the results.

---

## HEART HEALING

Are you willing to try a fresh activity that makes your juices flow? What colours are you showing people on a daily basis: are any of them dreary? Are you ready to embrace scarlet passion and express it to a partner or a lover in a way that you never have? If you don't have a lover, then discover how to excite yourself!

Maybe you see emerald-green energy that you need to embrace, allowing yourself time for self-reflection, regeneration and something new and surprising. Can peach help you feel the depth of your creativity and rediscover a dream or desire that is now worth pursuing? Perhaps it's white and gold that call you: white to purify and let go of the past and gold to start embracing your spiritual nature and truly shine.

Whatever you need, it's time to embrace the new and reinvent yourself in a manner that makes you want to jump out of bed in the morning and seize the day.

## 31.

# INTUITIVE HEART

## STEP INTO YOUR TRUE DESTINY

Dear heart, I know you are constantly receiving intuitive hunches about the most important steps I need to take in my life journey. I'm sorry that I often ignore you and allow my head to rule. I'm ready to start listening to you even though it terrifies me.

Please unite me with my divine essence and act as a channel that allows me to feel aliveness and a connection with love and the source of life. I am willing to follow your guidance and step into my true destiny. I am now strong enough to hear the truth and follow it even if it is not what I want to hear, so please, dear heart, do not hold back. I know that the time for honesty and change is now!

---

# HEART HEALING

Have your journal close by to record any insights. Place your hands on your heart and ask: 'How open am I to receiving honest messages about [state what it is]?' Tune in to any blockages between your heart and yourself in terms of the messages you are resisting.

Acknowledge any fear you may have around receiving messages that would cause you to make major changes in your life. Imagine the fear looks like dark, smoky energy, then take it out of your heart with your physical hands and imagine placing it into a purple flame. Visualise sending soft orange light of courage into your intuitive heart and also to the part of you that can hear the wisdom and act on it.

Place your left hand on your heart again and ask your heart to tell you what you need to hear. Record that message in your journal along with the steps you need to take to make progress.

# 32.

# LONGING HEART

## VALUE WHAT YOU HAVE AND MORE WILL APPEAR

Dear heart, I know you are tired of waiting, longing and pushing for things to happen. There is so much confusion flowing inside you. You know that things occur in divine timing, but you are wondering whether your most earnest desires are real or they are just a fantasy.

The truth is they are a bit of both. There are parts of you that are stuck in the past, where you dreamed of being loved in a perfect way.

However, you are being called to let go of your old illusions and be willing to allow yourself to grow and mature. Connect within and reflect on what you now have the confidence to explore, knowing that life and love come with ups and downs. No matter what age you are there is a great opportunity to learn, evolve and value what you already have.

Profound love is on your doorstep: are you willing to let it in?

## HEART HEALING

Record in your journal what your deepest heart's desires are in love, your career and general life. Read over them and ask yourself whether they are your present dreams or whether they are connected to the younger you or even your family. If those wishes were from your earlier years or your family, explore how much fantasy or pain they contain.

Rewrite those desires from a wiser, more mature you, then explore what percentage of your real dreams have already come true or where you are halfway towards your goals. From the space of valuing what you have already experienced, with all your deepest feelings visualise receiving your more-developed desire into your heart.

## 33.

# UNAVAILABLE HEART
## FACE PAINFUL EXPERIENCES AND HEAL

Dear heart, I know you have found it painful to connect with other hearts that were broken, shut down and frozen. In fact, by attempting to connect with a heart that can't reciprocate love and affection you have added to your prior scars. A heart that is unavailable to love, reach towards divinity, connect with others and discern is often a hurt heart.

If you have found yourself meeting or even living with unavailable people you need to look within and lovingly meet the part of your heart that has been wounded and has closed off from the various aspects and flavours of love. To heal and unlock your zeal for life you will have to face everything that love brings up, including rejection, fear of abandonment, loss, hurt and betrayal. You have an opportunity to befriend those painful experiences and discover an empowering point of view that will lead to healing.

Do not spend one more moment being unavailable to all the exquisite beauty, passion, ingenuity, surprises, bliss, evolution and discovery that life presents.

## HEART HEALING

Record in your journal what keeps your heart self-protected and shut down, then next to each aspect explore how you can transform your limitations into your greatest allies. Can you turn rejection into deep self-acceptance? Can you see that past abandonment can lead you to self-partnering and learning to take care of you? Can the loss of love and affection lead you towards deeper knowledge of yourself and an opportunity to meet someone who will love you in the ways you long to be loved?

You have a wise part inside of you that has learned from past trauma. This wise part of you can teach you to trust your inner wisdom and encourage you to learn healing tools, so that if you ever fall again you will have the means to pick yourself up.

## 34.

# DIVINELY CONNECTED HEART

## MEET YOUR KARMA

Dear heart, when you connect to the inner source of love and listen to your deeper wisdom life flows with ease and grace. Sublime energy envelops you and you start to have access to super-sensible insights. In order to keep filling your inner cup you need to give yourself more time to meditate on higher worlds and develop a deeper connection with your guardian angel. Just as you hold karmic threads of destiny in your hands, so do your angel and other exalted beings guide you towards higher wisdom and evolution.

The more you learn about your spiritual home the more clarity you will have on how everything is connected, including the difficult experiences that appear in your life. After all, when you are divinely connected, my dear heart, you understand that my spirit is eternal and has been through many earthly lives, thus there are karmic relationships that I must be able to face and work with in a new and more healing way than I may have done previously.

I urge you to embark on a spiritual quest, my divinely connected heart, so that together we can meet our karma with love, grace and wisdom.

## HEART HEALING

For the next several nights, before going to bed place your hands on your heart and call on your guardian angel, a master or a higher being that you connect with. Ask them to show you what you need to learn from your karmic destiny or karmic relationships. If any other questions arise, ask those then go to sleep. When you wake up, place your hands on your heart and ask to be shown any images, symbols or archetypes that can guide you. Record these. If you don't understand the symbolism ask to be shown it, but also do some research on the meaning.

# REJECTED HEART

### TRANSFORM HEARTBREAK
### INTO INNER STRENGTH

Dear heart, I know you have felt deeply rejected by the people you have been the most open, vulnerable and trusting with. You apprehensively revealed all of you, which felt scary and raw, yet you were willing to entrust yourself to another. However, rather than being nurtured, treasured and adored you were pushed away, ignored and excluded. The connection and understanding you longed for was severed.

You were met with coldness and at times cruelty, shattering what has already been cut into more pieces.

You keep trying to collect the pieces and place them into a protective shell so that you no longer have to feel the searing pain of being cast off, humiliated or ill-treated. I'm so sorry, dear heart, for the loss, neglect, manipulation and lack of care you have suffered, but the time has come for us to work together, collect the broken pieces and transform them into love, acceptance and healing. I am ready to see and value you, my dear heart, for all that you are.

## HEART HEALING

Close your eyes and connect with your heart. Ask to see an aspect that has been rejected that is now ready to receive healing. No matter what this part looks like, use your hands to gently caress it. In your own words, share how sorry you are for the pain that it has experienced. If this part had a voice, how would it respond to you? Let it express itself and patiently listen, then share from the wisest, most loving divine feminine part of you how you will help this aspect with self-love, acceptance, nurturing and expansion.

Visualise a beautiful, soft green light and imagine bathing your heart in this healing colour. Observe any changes that may take place. Thank everyone that has shown up and make a commitment to help your heart feel valued by you.

# 36.

# FORGIVING HEART

## DON'T LET THE PAST IMPRISON YOU IN THE PRESENT

Dear heart, as much as you have experienced a crushing sting of suffering and torment, the time has come to slowly and steadily let go of pain. Forgiveness doesn't mean that the callous treatment you experienced was justified; however, healing means that you can learn much from past pain and give yourself permission to move forward with a newfound wisdom and understanding.

Forgiveness asks you to no longer harbour or feed old painful trauma but instead move forward with more kindness towards yourself and others. Stop letting the past imprison you in the present. If you can't forgive the perpetrator of your suffering, then at least stop blaming yourself for putting yourself into a hostile situation.

If you are the one who carries guilt and grief about something you have done then take any possible steps to ask for forgiveness from someone else. Truly demonstrate to another that you have learned from the past and can be trustworthy in the present and the future.

---

## HEART HEALING

Place your hands on your heart and ask where there is still a charge, hidden blame, resentment or anger in your being over difficult experiences. Take some slow, deep breaths and acknowledge what you are feeling. Imagine there is a purple fire in front of you, then take any density you are ready to release out of your heart and place it into the purple fire.

Once you have let go, imagine a person that you can begin to forgive standing in front of you and say: 'I understand that you are an important part of my lessons in this life. I thank you for teaching me.' Take your time to say what it is and let them respond from their higher self, then come back to the present and journal anything else you need to express.

# ACKNOWLEDGEMENTS

I hope you will continue to enjoy working with this card deck and potentially combine it with my other decks, *Heal Yourself Reading Cards* and *Mystical Healing Reading Cards*, which are all complementary. I am deeply grateful for being able to turn the challenging experiences in my life into tools to help others. I encourage you to write love letters to different aspects of your heart, whenever difficult moments arise.

A big thank you to everyone who uses and shares my work with others.

I am forever grateful to my family, who are incredibly loving and supportive.

I have profound appreciation for Rockpool Publishing and the wonderful team I get to work with.

I also absolutely adored working with Jena Dellagrottaglia, who intuitively understood my crazy briefs and was able to create stunning images that speak to the heart.

# ABOUT THE AUTHOR

Inna Segal is the award-winning, bestselling author of *The Secret Language of Your Body: The essential guide to health and wellness*, *The Secret of Life Wellness: The essential guide to life's big questions*, *Understanding Modern Spirituality*, *Heal Yourself Reading Cards* and *Mystical Healing Reading Cards*. She has also created a variety of helpful healing audios and in-depth online programs.

Inna is an internationally recognised healer, teacher, professional speaker, author and pioneer in the field of energy medicine and human consciousness. Via intuitive means she can 'see' illness and blocks in a person's body, explain what is occurring and guide people through self-healing processes. However, her focus is not just on helping people heal physically but also helping them reconnect with their spiritual divine nature and understand deeper aspects of evolution.

When Inna was a teenager she suffered with severe back pain, anxiety and a skin disorder. In an incredible twist of fate, while meditating she was able to receive help from the divine source and unlock her ability to intuitively see into her body. By asking pertinent questions she was able to discover the root of her pain, release heavy energies and emotions and heal herself. This experience awakened her intuitive abilities to see what is happening in other people's bodies and inner lives.

Inna teaches her students how to understand the symbolic ways their bodies and souls communicate through metaphor, images, feelings, memories, colours, sensations, thoughts and symbols. Her mission is to help people to awaken their inner life and step onto their true path of wellness and creativity and acknowledge the gifts and abilities their spirit has brought to them.

Her books, cards and events (both live and online) are based on deep ancient wisdom combined with a modern understanding of what is needed right now to be our best selves, and the processes that allow us to grow and expand in a safe, profound and lasting manner. Her passion is to help people understand the hidden mysteries of our existence – in particular, where we came from, where we are at at the present moment and where we are going in our future incarnations. She deeply believes that we have to become more conscious of spiritual realities, which help us to understand the most progressive ways to live.

www.innasegal.com
Facebook @InnaSegalAuthor

# ABOUT THE ILLUSTRATOR

Jena Dellagrottaglia has been creating oracle and tarot decks for several years and with some of the most well-known authors and publishers. Through digital mediums Jena has designed over a dozen decks and has been featured in *Oprah Daily* and many other design outlets. Her artwork has been featured on creative furniture pieces as well as greeting cards and more. This deck is her first as both an author and artist and she is excited to create more!

www.autumnsgoddess.com
Instagram @Jena_dellagrottaglia